COMMUNITY · CONNECTIONS

?

HOW DO WE LIVE TOGETHER?
HAWKS

BY KATIE MARSICO

CHERRY LAKE Publishing

Published in the United States of America by Cherry Lake Publishing
Ann Arbor, Michigan
www.cherrylakepublishing.com

Content Adviser: Stephen S. Ditchkoff, PhD, Associate Professor, Forestry and
Wildlife Sciences, Auburn University
Reading Adviser: Cecilia Minden-Cupp, PhD, Literacy Consultant

Photo Credits: Cover and page 1, ©Ronnie Howard, used under license from Shutterstock, Inc.;
page 5, ©iStockphoto.com/HamidEbrahimi; page 7, ©Ron Rowan Photography, used under
license from Shutterstock, Inc.; page 9, ©Peter Weber, used under license from Shutterstock, Inc.;
page 11, ©iStockphoto.com/RollingEarth; page 13, ©iStockphoto.com/SteveByland; page 15,
©JJJ, used under license from Shutterstock, Inc.; page 17, ©William Leaman/Alamy; page 19,
©Steve Nudson/Alamy; page 21, ©iStockphoto.com/SteveMcsweeny

LIBRARY OF CONGRESS CATALOGING-IN-PUBLICATION DATA
Marsico, Katie, 1980–
  How do we live together? Hawks / by Katie Marsico.
    p. cm.—(Community connections)
  Includes bibliographical references and index.
  ISBN-13: 978-1-60279-624-9
  ISBN-10: 1-60279-624-6
  1. Hawks—Juvenile literature. I. Title. II. Title: Hawks. III. Series.
  QL696.F32M264 2010
  598.9'44—dc22   2009022121

Cherry Lake Publishing would like to acknowledge the
work of The Partnership for 21st Century Skills. Please
visit www.21stcenturyskills.org for more information.

Printed in the United States of America
Corporate Graphics Inc.
January 2010
CLSP06

HAWKS

CONTENTS

WHY ARE THE BIRDS SO QUIET?

Many birds gather at your family's backyard feeder. Everyone loves listening to the birds sing. Today it is quiet, though. You look outside and see the reason why. A hawk is sitting in a nearby tree. It has scared away the other birds!

Hawks have very good eyesight.

Hawks are **predators**. This means that they hunt and eat other animals. Hawks often go after smaller birds. They have even been known to attack small cats and dogs. But this does not happen very often.

Hawks hunt and eat many kinds of small animals.

Draw a picture of all
the animals that you
see in your backyard.
Do you ever notice
any hawks there?
Does your drawing
include pictures of
any other predators?

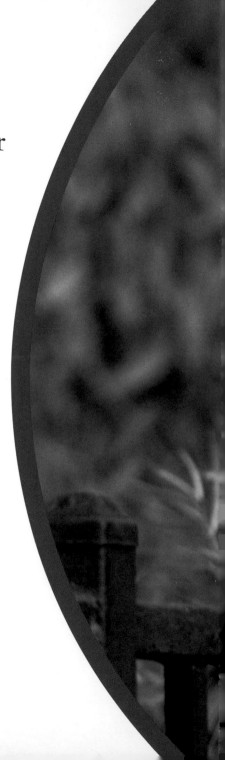

Some people do not like hawks. They are afraid one might hurt their pet. They also do not want hawks to chase away smaller birds that gather at backyard feeders. Other people enjoy watching these large predators.

How can we safely share our outdoor spaces with hawks? Understanding more about hawks can help.

Have you ever seen a hawk in your backyard?

A CLOSER LOOK AT HAWKS

Have you ever seen a hawk up close at a zoo or wildlife park? Did you notice its sharp claws? These are called **talons**. A hawk uses its talons to catch animals that it wants to eat. A hawk's hooked **beak** helps it tear its **prey** into smaller pieces.

A hawk's beak is very sharp.

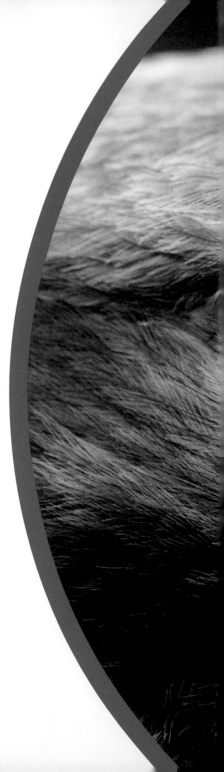

Hawks are found in most parts of the world. Many species **migrate** during the year. They usually travel to warmer places during cold seasons.

Hawks like to hunt for food in forests and grassy areas. They eat other birds, squirrels, and mice. They also eat rabbits, frogs, and snakes.

Hawks fly long distances when they migrate.

Hawks like areas where it is easy to find food. A backyard or farm can be the perfect place to find prey. Small animals are easier to spot in short grass and open spaces.

Many people enjoy watching birds at their backyard feeders. They don't want hawks to hunt the small birds that gather there.

THINK!

Can you think of any ways that hawks help humans? Think of what these predators eat. Mice can spread illnesses. Rabbits can damage plants and flowers. Hawks limit the number of mice and rabbits by hunting them for food.

SHARING OUTDOOR SPACES

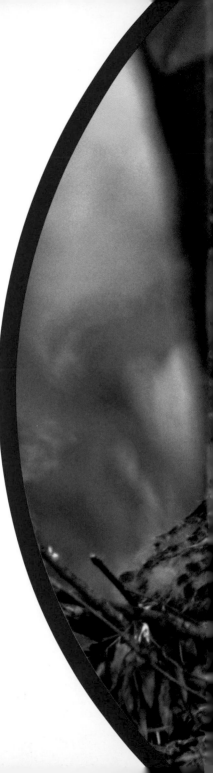

Hawks are wild animals. They need outdoor spaces to build homes and find food.

People often create areas in their backyards where it is easy for hawks to hunt. Look around your yard. Try to see it through the eyes of a hawk. What can you do to make your yard less inviting?

A hawk brings food back to the nest for its young.

17

17

Do you have a bird feeder? Take it down for a few weeks. Fewer birds will gather in your yard. Hawks that visit your yard may decide to move on.

What if you like to watch hawks? Place the feeder close to bushes. Then smaller birds will have a place to hide if a hawk is nearby.

Birdhouses and feeders are easy targets for hawks.

Ask an adult to help you contact wildlife experts. Wildlife experts can give you more information about hawks and other outdoor predators. They can explain ways to keep these animals from hunting in your yard.

What else can you do? Remember to respect the wildlife around you. The outdoors is their home. It is up to all of us. Let's share the outdoor community we call nature!

A flying hawk can be a beautiful sight!

GLOSSARY

beak (BEEK) the hard, curved mouthpart of birds

migrate (MYE-grate) to move from one place to another

predators (PRED-uh-turz) animals that hunt and kill other animals for food

prey (PRAY) animals that are hunted and eaten by other animals

talons (TAL-uhnz) the sharp, hooked claws of certain birds

FIND OUT MORE

BOOKS

Lundgren, Julie K. *Hawks*. Vero Beach, FL: Rourke, 2010.

McCarthy, Meghan. *City Hawk: The Story of Pale Male*. New York: Simon & Schuster Books for Young Readers, 2007.

WEB SITES

Animal Planet—Wild Animals A to Z: Hawk
animal.discovery.com/birds/hawk/
Visit this site for pictures and more facts about hawks and other birds of prey.

National Geographic Kids—Animals Creature Feature: Red-Tailed Hawks
kids.nationalgeographic.com/Animals/CreatureFeature/Red-tailed-hawk
Learn some interesting facts about red-tailed hawks.

INDEX

ABOUT THE AUTHOR

Katie Marsico is the author of more than 50 children's books and lives in Elmhurst, Illinois, with her husband and three children. She is sometimes visited by hawks in her own backyard.

24